I want to dedicate this book to
my mother
who not only did all this stuff
and so much more, thank you

WHEN GOD THOUGHT OF CHILDREN LIKE YOU AND I
HE THOUGHT ABOUT THE THINGS WE WOULD NEED. THINGS LIKE...

OUR DIAPERS BEING CHANGED

MAKING SURE WE WERE FED

SHOWING US HOW TO CRAWL

THEN CHEERING US ON AS WE TRIED TO WALK

AS WE
GREW
OLDER HE
ALSO
KNEW WE
WOULD
NEED
SOMEONE
WHO
WOULD...
STAR

TEACH US OUR ABC'S
AND OUR 123'S

ANSWER ALL OF OUR NEVER ENDING QUESTIONS
6

HE KNEW THE JOB WOULD NOT BE EASY, THAT WE WOULD NEED SOMEONE WHO WOULD...

HELP US WITH
OUR PROJECTS
AND
ASSIGNMENTS

HAVE THE GREATEST
TIME MANAGEMENT

SOMEONE WHO CAN MULTITASK,

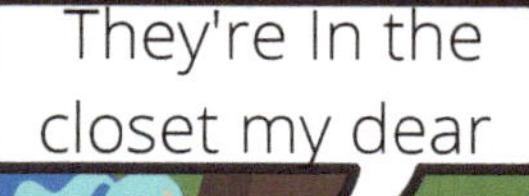

AND MIRACULOUSLY REMEMBER WHERE EVERYTHING IS AT IN THE HOUSE

HE KNEW IT NEEDED TO BE SOMEONE WHO LOVED US ENOUGH THAT THEY WOULD...

KNOW WHEN WE WERE
LYING TO STAY OUT OF
TROUBLE

SENSES WHEN WE ARE REALLY NOT
OKAY,
EVEN THOUGH WE SAY WE ARE

ALWAYS THERE FOR US,WHEN
WANTED, UNWANTED, AND MOST
DEFINITELY NEEDED
12

WHEN GOD THOUGHT ABOUT
ALL THESE THINGS THAT A
CHILD WOULD NEED...HE
THEN KNEW THE CREATION HE
NEEDED TO MAKE..

A super human!
14

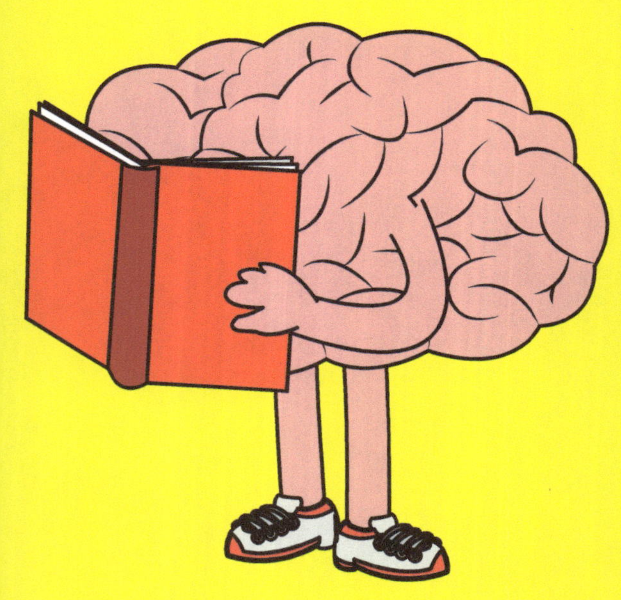

BUT NOT JUST ANY SUPER HUMAN, OH NO! THIS SUPER HUMAN NEEDED TO BE ABLE TO READ MINDS AND ALSO HAVE EYES IN THE BACK OF THEIR HEAD

15

SOMEONE WHO CAN COOK, CLEAN, AND HELP WITH HOMEWORK ALL AT THE SAME TIME

SOMEONE THAT GIVES YOU THE SAME AMOUNT OF LOVE AND JUST A LITTLE MORE EACH AND EVERYDAY

GOD KNEW IT WOULD BE A CHALLEGING AND HONORABLE JOB, MOST DEFINETLY NOT FOR THE WEAK
18

THAT IS
WHEN HE
ROLLED UP
HIS
SLEEVES
AND GAVE
US THE BEST
THING
SINCE
SLICED
BREAD..

MOTHERS